Then and Now

Contents

Rigby

Life Long Ago

Things were very different 200 years ago. There were no cars, buses, or airplanes.

There were no telephones, TVs, or electricity for lights and other things. What if you lived 200 years ago? How would your life **then** have been different from your life **now**?

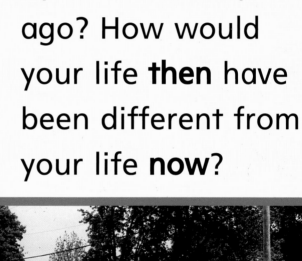

Homes Then

Many homes had one main room. The room had a large fireplace for cooking and heat. The family had to go outside to get water from a well.

Homes Now

Most homes have many rooms. We cook in the kitchen. A furnace heats our home. Pipes bring water inside our home.

Clothes Then

Most clothes were made by hand. The clothes were simple in color and style. Girls wore long dresses. Only boys wore pants.

Clothes Now

We buy many of our clothes at stores. They come in many colors and styles. Girls can choose to wear pants or dresses.

Food Then

People had to hunt for meat. They grew their own grains, fruits, and vegetables. There was no way to keep food fresh.

Food Now

We buy much of our food from grocery stores. Some people still grow vegetables in gardens. We can keep food longer because we have refrigerators and freezers.

Travel Then

People rode on horses and in wagons to get where they were going. It could take months to visit people who lived far away.

Travel Now

We ride in cars, buses, trains, and airplanes. We can travel many miles in just a few hours.

School Then

Schools were just one room. One teacher taught all the grades together. There were only a few books and school supplies.

School Now

Most schools have many classrooms. Different teachers teach different grades. There are a lot more books and school supplies.

Playtime Then

Many toys were made by hand.
Children played games with marbles
and had fun on stilts. They also
played tag and hide-and-seek.

Playtime Now

We buy most of our toys from stores. We play games on computers, but we still enjoy tag and hide-and-seek. Some things don't change.

Index

a
b
c
d
e
f
g
h
i
j
k
l
m
n
o
p
q
r
s
t
u
v
w
x
y
z